THE ESSENTIAL
MACHIAVELLI

THE
ESSENTIAL
MACHIAVELLI

Paul Strathern

This edition first published in Great Britain in 2002 by
Virgin Books Ltd
Thames Wharf Studios
Rainville Road
London
W6 9HA

First published in the USA in 1998 as *Machiavelli in 90 Minutes* by Ivan R Dee

A catalogue record for this book is available from the British Library.

ISBN 0 7535 0613 0

Typeset by TW Typesetting, Plymouth, Devon
Printed and bound in Great Britain by
Clays Ltd, St Ives PLC

CONTENTS

CONTENTS

THE ESSENTIAL
MACHIAVELLI

INTRODUCTION

Machiavelli's name sends a shiver down the spine. More than 350 years after his death it remains almost synonymous with evil. Yet Machiavelli was not an evil man. And as we shall see, his political philosophy was not evil *in itself*. It was just extremely realistic.

Our reaction says something about us rather than about Machiavelli. The philosophy of statecraft that he put forward aimed at being scientific. This meant there was no room for sentiment or compassion – or even, ultimately, morality.

Machiavelli's masterpiece, the single short work for which he will always be remembered, is *The Prince*. This is a book of advice to a prince on how to run his state. It is highly rational, psychologically perceptive, and addresses the heart of the matter with no nonsense. If you are a prince running a state, your chief aim is to remain in power and run your state to your best advantage. Machiavelli sets down how to do this, using a wealth of historical examples, and with a complete lack of sentimentality. No pussyfooting about: here's the formula.

Machiavelli's political philosophy intimately reflects his life, times, and circumstances. Most of his life was spent deeply involved in the politics of Renaissance Italy. As his life progresses, we see the lineaments of his philosophy beginning to emerge, feature by feature, until suddenly he falls from grace and is stripped of all that he considers to be his life. Bereft, and in complete despair, he sits down and writes his masterpiece, *The Prince*. In just a few months of supreme inspiration, he delivers himself of his entire political philosophy, complete and intact. Its harshness reflects the harshness of the political life he has seen, as well as the harshness of the blow he has just experienced. But this is more than just a political philosophy of its time. Machiavelli's thought pinpoints a central aspect of the political philosophy of all time – from Alexander the Great to Saddam Hussein. And as we shall see, it also reflects one of the most profound, and profoundly disturbing, truths of the human condition.

MACHIAVELLI'S LIFE AND WORKS

Niccolò Machiavelli was born in Florence on 3 May 1469. He came from an old Tuscan family, which had in the past achieved some eminence – though this was not one of the great powerful families of Florence, such as the Pazzi bankers or the Medici. And by the time Niccolò arrived on the scene, his branch of the family had fallen on hard times.

Machiavelli's father Bernardo was a lawyer who had fallen foul of the tax man and been declared an insolvent debtor. As such he was forbidden by law from practising his profession. But no lawyer can be expected to take the law literally. Bernardo managed to practise on the quiet, offering cut-rate service for those who found themselves in an impecunious position similar to his own. His only other source of income was the small estate he had inherited, seven miles south of Florence on the road to Siena. This was an idyllic spot amidst the Tuscan hills, but the grapes and goat cheese hardly provided enough cash to support a family. Life was austere at *casa* Machiavelli. As Niccolò later remarked: 'I learned to do without before I learned to enjoy.' Bernardo could afford no formal education for his son. Occasionally a scholar on hard times would be hired as a tutor. But Bernardo had not always been a broken-down lawyer. He had his own library, and young Niccolò was soon reading extensively, especially in classical texts. The pale, deprived boy found his imagination fired by the wonders of ancient Rome.

The isolated child gave way to a solitary adolescent with an apprehensive, sidelong look, which made him appear curiously guilty. He became aware of the world around him: coolly measuring himself against it, measuring it against what he knew from his reading. Even in his isolation he couldn't help realising his superior intelligence. Likewise, he quickly perceived the new humanist outlook that was beginning to permeate so many aspects of the city around him. Florence was emerging from the intellectual torpor of medieval life: the city felt awake, alive, self-confident. Italy was leading Western civilisation into the Renaissance. It was possible to dream that Italy might again be united and great, as it had been in the days of the Roman Empire. The perceptive young Niccolò began seeing (and imagining) resemblances between the city around him and Rome at the height of its power: the Rome of the second century AD, in the era leading up to Marcus Aurelius, stoic philosopher, general, emperor. This was the period when the empire stretched from the Persian Gulf to Hadrian's Wall, when the Senate still had sufficient power to make itself heard, when the citizens of Rome had been happiest and most prosperous. Heady stuff for a quicksilver young mind whose broken father could provide no role model. Instead, history would provide a more abstract dream.

Machiavelli's understanding of the heyday of the Roman Empire was not clouded by the rhetoric of an erudite teacher. Yet he certainly attended some of the public lectures given by the great humanist scholars who were then making Florence the intellectual centre of Europe. Characteristic of these was the poet and humanist Politian, protégé and close friend of Lorenzo the Magnificent. Politian was one of the finest poets of the post-Dante era, his verse combining rhetorical flourishes of classical brilliance with the directness and vivacity of everyday Florentine Italian. The scholars at the University of Florence quickly learned how to mimic this elegant poesy. Unhampered by intellectual fashion, Machiavelli began turning this same Florentine Italian into a more clear and direct prose, combining formal manner with popular usage. The Italian language was in its infancy. It had evolved from Florentine dialect less than two centuries earlier, displacing Latin as the literary language. Yet it had already produced its greatest poet (Dante), and in Machiavelli it was now about to produce its finest prose writer.

After the public lectures the young scholars would linger in the Piazza della Signoria, swapping opinions, the latest news on the affairs of the day, gossip. The cool young man with the snide look was soon noticed. His ironic barbs, his witticisms (especially at the expense of the clergy), his piercing intellectual insights, all made their mark. Just as he intended they should. Niccolò knew what he was doing: he was establishing himself. (And almost without realising it, he was also creating himself.) He may have had only modest social standing, but he knew he was better than any of them. His mockery provided a suitable mask for such contemptuous conceit. And in his own way Machiavelli soon established himself as the life and soul of the party. The way to succeed was to win popularity. Only the more perceptive among his friends noticed the cool heart that lay behind the mask. Either through pity, respect, or curiosity, this often endeared him to them all the more. A cool heart was a rare phenomenon among the volatile young bloods of Renaissance Florence.

But how was it that Florence, of all places, had become the centre of the Renaissance? Here was a city with little political or military clout, yet it had achieved an influence out of all proportion to its provincial standing.

The obvious answer is money. The Florentine merchant bankers, such as the Medici, Pazzi, and Strozzi families, controlled the new technology of their age. Merchant banking was the revolutionary communication technology of its time. Its development during the fourteenth century had gradually transformed trade and communication throughout Europe.

Wealth could be transmitted, in the form of credit or bank drafts, from one end of the continent to another, freeing trade from the customary restraints of barter or cash payment. Silks and spices arriving overland from the Far East at Beirut could be purchased by means of financial transfer and shipped to Venice.

The second oldest profession is the middleman, and one of the invariable rules of money-handling is that some of it always adheres to each hand through which it passes. Sealskins and whale oil, shipped from Greenland to Brugge, could be used to pay papal dues, which could then be transferred by banker's draft to the Vatican in Rome. And here lay the heart of the matter. Papal revenues were extracted from parishes, dioceses, and rulers throughout Christendom – which, regardless of national borders, then stretched from Portugal to Sweden, from Greenland to Cyprus. Only the greatest banking houses, with trusted branches along the trade routes throughout Europe, could handle the transfer of such widespread income, from its far-flung sources, along the converging tributaries, to its ultimate mouth. Inevitably there was great competition for this prize account, involving all the usual skills associated with great banking enterprises: political chicanery, bribery, creative accounting, and so forth. And by 1414 the Medici had finally secured the big one: they were the papal bankers. Similar manoeuvres enabled the Medici family to gain control of the ostensibly democratic republican government of Florence. By 1434 Cosimo de' Medici was not only the richest man in Europe, but Florence had become his own private princedom in all but name.

The city now flourished as never before, achieving international renown. The local coin, the florin (named after the city), became the dollar of its day. Among the chaos of European coinage (where countries frequently had several different currencies in circulation), the florin was recognised as the international monetary standard. Similarly, financial transaction played its role in establishing the Florentine dialect as the Italian language. Money soon bred a self-confidence that cast aside the traditional medieval outlook, ignoring the intellectual stranglehold of the church. Biblical homilies concerning wealth ('It is easier for a rich man to pass through the eye of a needle than to enter heaven', etc.) were reinterpreted in the light of current reality: the pages of the Medici banking ledgers were blatantly headed: 'In the name of God and profit.'

But cash alone didn't account for Florence's pre-eminence. It was how the cash was spent. The Medicis' close association with the church gave them access to the intimate workings of this flourishing commercial organisation (even cardinals had bank accounts devoted purely to expenditure on their mistresses). Despite such disillusioning disclosures, the Medici remained firm and unquestioning believers in Christianity. Yet the fact remained that the central function of banking – namely, usury – was expressly and unequivocally forbidden by the Bible. ('Thou shalt not lend thy money for interest.' Leviticus 24:37. 'Do not take usury.' Exodus 22:25, and so on and so forth.)

As Cosimo de' Medici became older, he became increasingly perturbed. To assuage his guilt (and perhaps buy himself a lesser period of hellfire and damnation) he began lavishing extravagant sums on refurbishing churches, building new ones, and decorating them with the finest works of art. The Medici became the greatest private patrons of the arts the world has ever seen. Painting, architecture, literature, scholarship – all flourished as a result of Medici beneficence.

The new humanist self-confidence and generous patronage combined with, and encouraged, a resurgence in the learning of ancient Greece and Rome. This was the real Renaissance (literally 'rebirth'). During the Middle Ages the remnants of classical learning that had survived in Europe had become smothered in the teachings of Scholasticism, the original texts obscured by centuries of Christian 'interpretation'. But other texts that had survived in the Middle East now began reaching Europe. Their clarity and learning came as a revelation. Philosophy, the arts, architecture, mathematics, literature – all were to be transformed by this rebirth of ancient knowledge. Our entire way of seeing the world was transformed. Existence was no longer just an endurance test in preparation for the next world, it was an arena in which one displayed one's skills. The young Machiavelli lapped it up. Here was his opportunity. He would see life as it is, not as it ought to be.

Meanwhile Florence began attracting the finest talents in Italy, which at the time was culturally the most advanced country in Europe. During the latter years of the fifteenth century, Michelangelo, Raphael, and Botticelli all worked in Florence. Minds of the calibre of Leonardo were attracted to the city. And Florence gave, too: among Machiavelli's friends was Amerigo Vespucci, who was to become an early explorer of the New World (which is called after his Christian name). The great future historian of Italy, Francesco Guicciardini, was also a friend, and together he and Machiavelli attended public lectures given by the greatest Renaissance philosopher of them all, the dazzlingly brilliant Pico della Mirandola, another protégé of Lorenzo the Magnificent. Pico challenged the finest minds in Europe to debate his conclusions with him when, at just twenty-three, he achieved the accolade of being accused of heresy by the pope himself, and was to die at just thirty-one. Machiavelli was not alone in admiring Pico, whom Michelangelo referred to as 'a man almost divine'. Pico's orations and treatises on such subjects as human dignity are the epitome of Renaissance thought. They succeed in combining Christian theology, the finest elements of classical philosophy, and curious remnants of hermetic thinking (such as alchemy, magic, and ideas from the Cabala). On the other hand, his thinking was often highly scientific. And his attack on astrology (in fact, from a religious point of view) was to have a formative effect on the seventeenth-century astronomer Johannes Kepler in his ideas on planetary motion.

This curious mixture of Christian theology, classical thought, embryonic scientific attitude, and medieval magic was typical of contemporary thinking. The Renaissance marks the definitive break between the Middle Ages and the Age of Reason. It straddles both eras, and many of the finest minds of this period contained elements of both ages. Shakespeare's world, for instance, is intoxicated with a heady brew of humanistic individualism and medieval superstition. (Not for nothing did classical French taste regard him as a barbarian until well into the nineteenth century.) Likewise, the new science of chemistry relied for its methodology upon the techniques of alchemy.

Machiavelli was to be something of an exception here. Possibly owing to his self-education, he retained a mind of his own. His writings were to be largely (and scandalously) free of illusion or superstition, though his letters reveal that he did subscribe, perhaps semi-ironically, to the usual nonsense of astrology and current Florentine superstitions.

The apotheosis of Renaissance Florence was achieved under Lorenzo the Magnificent, who reigned from 1478 until the year Columbus reached America. Lorenzo the Magnificent was the grandson of Cosimo de' Medici, by then known as *pater patriae* (father of the country). Lorenzo undoubtedly lived up to his appendage. Statesman, patron of the arts, and poet, his achievement in any one of these spheres would have ensured him a place in Italian history. The citizens of Florence appreciated the greatness he was bringing to their city, and he in turn encouraged a resplendent, carefree atmosphere with regular carnivals, spectacular processions, and tournaments. The perceptive Guicciardini described Lorenzo as 'a benevolent tyrant in a constitutional republic'.

Yet beneath the surface glitter Florentine society retained its darker side: bitter scheming and a testosterone-fuelled social volatility. The peacock costumes of silk hose and velveteen doublets were worn with daggers and swords. These may have been for show (as Freud would have recognised), but they were not merely ornamental. Eruptions of sudden and deadly violence were all too frequent.

Machiavelli himself would certainly have witnessed the worst of these: the so-called Pazzi Conspiracy. This occurred in 1478, just after the Pazzi family had managed to take over as papal bankers. (Lorenzo was as magnificent a spender as his grandfather had been a saver: even his most loyal supporters recognised that he was temperamentally not cut out to be a bank manager.) Having taken over the main money supply, the Pazzi were now determined to take over Florence as well.

The Pazzi family hatched a plot to assassinate Lorenzo and his younger brother Giuliano during Easter Mass, while their confederate, the archbishop of Pisa, was to occupy the Palazzo Vecchio, the seat of the elected council and the gonfalonier (the official elected ruler of the city). Members of the Medici and Pazzi families headed the Easter procession, mingling casually arm in arm as they entered the cathedral. On the given signal (the elevation of the Host by the priest), the Pazzis abruptly unsheathed their daggers. Giuliano was stabbed to death before the altar, one of his assassins attacking him in such a frenzy that he plunged his knife into his own leg and was unable to take further part in the proceedings. At the same time Lorenzo frantically defended himself with his sword while his companion Politian came to his aid. The intervention of his poet-friend saved Lorenzo's life, and he managed to escape into the sacristy with only a slice-wound to the neck.

Meanwhile, less than a quarter of a mile away in the Palazzo Vecchio the other part of the plot was unfolding. The archbishop of Pisa, dressed in full episcopal regalia, set off upstairs to the council chamber, followed unobtrusively by the other Pazzi conspirators. He encountered the gonfalonier, who immediately became suspicious and called the guards. The archbishop was seized and questioned. As soon as the gonfalonier discovered what was happening, he peremptorily ordered the archbishop to be hung. The cleric was bound and flung out the window in full episcopal regalia with a rope around his neck. A moment later his leading Pazzi confederate was flung out after him, also with a rope around his neck. The jeering crowd below watched as the two bound men dangled from the overhanging window, desperately biting into each other in an attempt to save themselves. In the distance could be heard a baying chorus from outside the cathedral, as the crowd tore the remaining conspirators apart limb from limb.

The effect of such a scene on the young Machiavelli can only be imagined. He had witnessed history, an event that would never be forgotten. It was quick, decisive, and horrific. And victory went to the one who had acted quickest, most decisively, and most horrifically. (Do unto others as they would do unto you – but do it first, and do it conclusively.) Such was Machiavelli's formative political education.

But even the Florentines were eventually to tire of such sensational public entertainments. The popularity of the Medici waned, and external events inflicted serious defeats. In 1494, just two years after the death of Lorenzo the Magnificent, the Medici lost control and were forced to flee the city. This event was precipitated by the entry of the French king Charles VIII and his victorious troops into Florence, an unheard-of event. Although the occupation of Florence by

Charles VIII proved largely symbolic, and ended in a few days, it marked a new phase in Florentine politics. Wars had become serious: the city was in danger of losing its independence to a foreign power. Standing among the silent crowds as Charles VIII rode in triumph through the streets, his lance held high, Machiavelli felt deeply shamed to see his city so humiliated. He felt shame as a Florentine and shame as an Italian. Here was yet another formative political lesson taking place before his eyes. (Only a united Italy could repel the might of the French.)

With the Medici gone, Florence now fell under the influence of the firebrand priest Savonarola, who railed against the corruption of the papacy (a rich source indeed for sermons on the frailties of the flesh). The Ayatollah Khomeini of his day, Savonarola introduced a regime of hellfire sermons and hell-on-earth abstinence. The joyous days of festivals and spectacular assassination attempts were over. Savonarola instituted 'the bonfire of the vanities'. Citizens surrendered their fine artworks and fine attire to the blazing pyre (though they prudently withheld their finest artworks and finest attire for another day).

Savonarola's Christian Republic was to last four years (1494–1498). Even the delicate *primavera* magic of Botticelli succumbed to leaden biblical agonies. Then it was Savonarola's turn for the bonfire, and he achieved the martyrdom that was his due. Machiavelli would have witnessed this gruesome event too. More history in the raw, from which to draw his own lesson.

In 1498 the moderate Soderini was elected gonfalonier of Florence, and for the first time Machiavelli emerges from the shadows. His great Italian biographer Villari invokes the 29-year-old Machiavelli as a rather unprepossessing, not to say curious, figure. Slender, beady eyes, black hair, small head, aquiline nose, and tightly closed mouth. And yet, 'everything about him conveyed the impression of a very acute observer and sharp mind, though not someone who was liable to influence people much'. Villari mentions his 'sarcastic expression', 'air of cold and inscrutable calculation', and 'powerful imagination'. Not exactly a person one warms to. Yet Machiavelli must have impressed a number of influential people. Even before the fall of Savonarola he was proposed as a candidate for secretary to the Second Chancery, that is, in charge of the committee dealing with foreign affairs. In the event, he was defeated by voters from the Savonarola faction. But when Soderini took over Florence, Machiavelli succeeded in gaining the post. A short time later he was voted in as secretary of the Ten of War, the committee that dealt with military affairs. These were to become increasingly important posts over the following years – something about this cool, clever, somewhat shifty figure evidently appealed to Soderini.

Machiavelli may have appeared shifty, but he was in fact extremely loyal. This and his dispassionate intellect were to prove rare virtues in the passionate, devious world of Italian politics. Soderini had recognised someone who could size up a situation and see it for what it was.

Machiavelli was soon being sent on diplomatic business to the courts of nearby city-states. The secretary of the Second Chancery would be entrusted with errands and negotiations that were not considered sufficiently important for an ambassador heading an official mission. He began cutting his teeth on the intricacies of diplomatic intrigue, sending back clear reports with frank assessments. Despite the usual entrapments and enticements, he demonstrated his talents with considerable skill. Here was that rarity: a slippery customer you could trust. Here indeed was a man who was loyal, though only to his friends and his city. In other spheres the appearance mirrored the man – to suitably impressive effect.

Within a couple of years Machiavelli was given his first important mission: to the court of the French king Charles

VIII. The outcome of this mission was vital to the safety of Florence. By the end of the fifteenth century the divided and constantly squabbling city-states of central Italy were threatened from two sides. From the north they lay at the mercy of France, which saw the prospect of extending its territory deep into the Italian peninsula. In the south the powerful kingdom of Naples, ruled by the Spanish, had similar territorial ambitions. In order to survive, Florence had to perform a delicate balancing act.

During five months in France in 1500, Machiavelli observed first-hand the political setup of a large and powerful European nation, united under the rule of a single leader. His mission was inconclusive – that is, successful. (Florence tentatively remained an ally; France didn't swallow it up. Yet.)

Machiavelli returned to Florence in 1501, where he was married to Marietta di Luigi Corsini, who came from a family of similar social standing. (But the Corsinis had managed to hang on to a bit more of their money than the Machiavellis, and could thus provide a reasonable dowry.) As was the custom of the period, this was no love match. The marriage was a largely social affair, linking two families in a useful alliance. Fortunately Niccolò and Marietta hit it off and were soon good friends.

Machiavelli always retained a deep affection for his wife, and they were to have five children. As far as we can judge from her letters, Marietta reciprocated Niccolò's affection. Such arranged marriages frequently developed into deep friendship, involving a mutual respect and consideration which is prone to wither amidst the more combustible expectations of romantic love. But this was very much a one-sided arrangement, characteristic of the country and the period. When he was on a mission for any length of time in a foreign city, Machiavelli would usually form a relationship with an unattached lady. And judging from his letters to male friends, he formed a gentle affection for these partners too, as they did for him. (In their replies, his friends would tease him on this point.) No correspondence concerning Marietta's love life has fallen into the hot hands of history. And if the existence of such a life had even been suspected, the consequences for Marietta would have been dire indeed. (Those for her correspondent don't even bear thinking about.) Italian attitudes to such matters remained open-ended, but only at one end. This single-minded attitude towards relationships was also to inform Machiavelli's political philosophy. (For a ruler there could be no equal relationships. The senior partner enforced the rules but remained free to act in his own interest.)

Florence now faced a new threat. The pope's son, the notorious Cesare Borgia, was using the papal army (aided by French troops) to carve out a new independent principality for himself in central Italy. As Borgia marched north from Rome, conquering territories as far afield as Rimini on the Adriatic coast, the entire region was in ferment.

In an attempt to stabilise the Florentine territories, Soderini was elected gonfalonier for life – an unprecedented move in a city that so prided itself on its republicanism. (Even the Medicis had only ruled *through* the elected gonfaloniers.)

Machiavelli was dispatched on a series of missions to report on uprisings in the Florentine territories, and as ambassador to the Borgia military headquarters (a position equivalent to an accredited resident spy). On the day before his arrival, Borgia had seized the strategic city of Urbino in a lightning coup. Machiavelli was dazzled by the brilliance of Borgia's ruthless tactics.

One of Machiavelli's reports to Florence concerned 'How to Deal with the Rebels in the Val di Chiana'. In this he showed that political philosophy was already central to his thinking: 'Especially for princes, history is an instruction manual on how to act . . . Human beings have always had the same passions and behaved in the same way . . . There have always been those who commanded, and those who obeyed, some willingly, others against their will . . .' Hardly insights of genius – but the lack of illusion is plain enough. Right from the start, Machiavelli delighted in putting forward what he considered to be universal historical laws. Out of these apparently unexceptional pebbles of knowledge he would ultimately construct his all but impregnable political fortress. But such a fortress needs a prince to occupy it. Significantly, even in this early work, Machiavelli remarks: 'Borgia possesses one of the attributes of great men: he is a shrewd opportunist and knows when to use the main chance to his best advantage.' (Ironically, Machiavelli's insight here is sharpened by the realisation that Borgia has his eyes on Florence.)

Machiavelli was to undertake a second mission to Cesare Borgia, which lasted from October 1502 until January 1503. This time he witnessed the horrific vengeance Borgia wreaked on some of his rebellious commanders. The incident forms the basis of Machiavelli's essay 'The Treachery of Duke Valentino [Borgia] Toward Vitelli and Others', which was worked up from his original eyewitness report.

The taking of Urbino had left Borgia in a powerful position – too powerful, in the opinion of his commander Vitelli and several senior officers. Mistrustful of Borgia's ruthlessness, they broke from him, allying themselves with his enemies. This left Borgia with only the remnants of his army. He immediately engaged in a defensive campaign in order to protect his possessions and buy time. Meanwhile he sequestered vast sums from the papal exchequer in order to build a powerful new army, at the same time embarking on diplomatic manoeuvres to divide his enemies, separating Vitelli and his co-conspirators from their allies. Vitelli soon saw which way the wind was blowing and decided to throw in his lot once more with Borgia. A reconciliation was duly arranged at the small town of Senigallia on the Adriatic coast. Borgia dismissed his French troops so as to reassure Vitelli and the others, turning up at Senigallia with a skeleton force. Here he welcomed Vitelli and his commanders 'with a pleasant countenance . . . greeting them like old friends'. As he did so, he manoeuvred them so that they were separated from their troops – whereupon he had them bundled off and flung into a dungeon. That night, as they 'wept and begged for mercy, frantically blaming each other', Borgia had them strangled.

This incident proved inspirational to Machiavelli. (It was later to play an exemplary role in *The Prince*, where it stars in Chapter 7 and is referred to on several other occasions.) Indeed, according to Villari, it was this incident and these months spent in the company of Cesare Borgia that gave Machiavelli the idea of 'a science of statecraft separate from, and independent of, every moral consideration'. What Machiavelli described in 'The Treachery of Duke Valentino Toward Vitelli and Others' was realpolitik.

Yet we should not mistake his description of this realpolitik for reality. Machiavelli was an artist who believed in the skilful embodiment of his ideas. Borgia did not in fact dismiss his French troops in order to reassure Vitelli – they were suddenly recalled, leaving Borgia badly exposed. He had no alternative but to bluff his way through his plan. (Machiavelli's delegation accompanied Borgia on this fateful trip, and his original report tellingly describes how the news of the French flight 'turned this court's brains topsy-turvy'. Likewise, all the weeping and blaming as the victims were strangled was also an embellishment. No mention of this was made in the original report. Machiavelli's intention was to heighten and deepen the character of Borgia, not to make the embodiment of his ideas appear a panicky cheat.)

Machiavelli's essays and *descrizione* are intended to convey his evolving political philosophy. Many of these pieces are marred by his insistence upon pointing out 'universal historical laws'. But his writings remain filled with a wealth of historical examples and vivid incidents, ranging from contemporary affairs which he himself has witnessed, to celebrated events from ancient Rome. The facts never simply buttress the theory, they bring it to life. That these facts are not always facts should not necessarily be allowed to detract from the theory. Machiavelli's political philosophy has its own power and conviction. But what precisely is this theory?

As yet, Machiavelli had but an inkling of what it would become (some kind of science independent of morals, as Villari suggests). Yet it seems he already had a developing subconscious idea. For the moment this remained inarticulate, its methodology little more than a hardening attitude, an unexpressed conviction. Machiavelli was learning to understand his philosophy by understanding its embodiment. For the time being, Cesare Borgia *was* Machiavelli's philosophy.

Like many an intellectual before and since, Machiavelli was spellbound by the ruthless man of action. Cesare Borgia was a stereotype of the dashing monster – a species which has rather gone out of fashion in our modern era of angst-ridden führers and dour peasant genocides. Borgia was no ordinary 'life-destroyer'.

The Borgias were of Spanish descent. This fact accounted for their dark seam of cruelty and vicious depravity, according to one of the great nineteenth-century Renaissance historians (writing in a period of prodigious scholarship and racism). Cesare Borgia's father became Pope Alessandro VI in 1492 by simply buying the papacy – possibly the first, though certainly not the last, time this occurred. Alessandro was temperamentally unsuited to the celibacy required of his calling. His many offspring included Cesare, Juan (the pope's favourite son), and his sister Lucrezia, legendary both as a poisoner and entertainer at orgies in the Vatican. (Lucrezia's illegitimate son was fathered by her father the pope, or possibly by Cesare – even they weren't sure which.) Cesare established himself as his father's favourite by the simple expedient of murdering the previous occupant of this role, his brother Juan. Whereupon he usurped Juan's other role as commander of the papal armies. This enabled him to launch his campaign to carve out a large private princedom for himself in central Italy. And so it went on.

The man whom Machiavelli observed at close quarters was a dangerous parody. 'The handsomest man in Italy', he was capable of captivating charm, possessed of indefatigable energy, capable of rousing his men with displays of finely judged rhetoric and bombastic brilliance, a military tactician of genius, a politician of polished panache. But this Renaissance prince of light was also a prince of manic-depressive darkness. Secretive, devious, liable to violent and unpredictable rages, prone for days on end to taciturn despairs when none dared rouse him from his darkened room.

Such a man appeared to Machiavelli to be capable of anything. Nothing could stop him as long as he didn't weaken or soften his approach in any way – as long as he followed the science of how to succeed, without regard for pity or morality . . . Yes, there *was* a method to his inspired madness. And Borgia knew how to use it.

In 1503 Alessandro VI died, and the pope who succeeded him was a sworn enemy of the Borgias. Cesare Borgia was arrested and flung into a dungeon. Allowed out only after he had forsworn his conquests, he fled to Naples, was arrested again and shipped to Spain in chains, then escaped his castle-prison to far-off France. Machiavelli watched as the stature of his hero diminished: the amoral giant among men reduced to a common fugitive. Machiavelli was baffled – repelled yet intrigued. The spellbound scholar gave way to the analysing intellectual. In his mind he now began to draw a distinction between the man and his methods. He pronounced his former hero to be 'a man without compassion, rebellious to Christ . . . deserving of the most wretched end'. But his methods were another matter. They had been science, an entirely new science, the science of politics.

Meanwhile Italian politics continued its kaleidoscope of alliances and betrayals. The Florentine republic remained under threat – not least from the Medicis, who had begun to rally support for their reinstatement as masters of the city. Despite being secretary for the Ten of War, and thus the leading figure in Florentine military affairs, Machiavelli had no actual military experience. (The Florentines had long ago wisely decided that such matters were best not left in the hands of military men.) Daringly, Machiavelli chose to put one of Cesare Borgia's ideas into practice. He decided that Florence should recruit its own militia from among its citizens and the territories under its control. Although Borgia had already tried this idea in Urbino, Machiavelli's initiative was greeted as a controversial new approach. The long-established Italian tradition of using mercenaries to fight their wars was now beginning to break down with the introduction of disciplined French and Spanish armies who actually fought for their country. The mercenaries had been accustomed to fighting each other – today's defender for Milan could well be alongside you in the attack for Florence next season. Thus there was no sense in anyone being put out of a job with unnecessary injuries or massacres.

In 1499 Machiavelli had experienced all this first-hand on a military mission to the Florentine forces besieging Pisa. Their mercenary commander had simply refused to attack the city on the grounds that it was dangerous.

Machiavelli received the support of the Florentine government for his plan to set up a militia, and embarked on a recruiting campaign. The new army went into training, and in recognition of its vital role a powerful new committee was set up to direct its affairs. With the encouragement of Soderini, Machiavelli was voted as secretary to this new committee.

Machiavelli and Soderini were now working hand in hand to ensure the safety of Florence. But events conspired against them. Pisa rebelled once more, cutting off Florentine access down the river Arno to the sea. The new militia of locals and ne'er-do-wells had not yet been forged into a fighting force sufficient to take a city. What was to be done?

Machiavelli turned to his chief military engineer, a white-bearded sage who had recently been transferred from Borgia's team to Florence. (Machiavelli had become friends with this interesting character during his mission to Borgia, and had spent several happy evenings discussing ideas over chianti, after their host had retired to plot.) The military engineer came up with a sensational idea, whose drastic originality fired Machiavelli's imagination.

The plan was to alter the course of the river Arno, no less, divert it into a lake – and then speedily dig a canal cross-country to the coast at Livorno. At a stroke, Pisa would be deprived of its water, its access to the sea, its hold over Florence. And the project could be achieved by just two thousand men in fifteen days 'if they were given sufficient inducement to work hard'.

Machiavelli, and soon Soderini too, were entranced by this plan hatched by their hired sage, whose name was Leonardo da Vinci. Work started on the project – and continued for two months. At this point the forces of sanity intervened. The ruling council in Florence recognised the plan as 'little better than a fantasy' and ordered it abandoned.

Here Machiavelli had revealed another trait which was to play a formative role in his political philosophy. The cool observant intellectual was not only a sucker for the larger-than-life character (as in Borgia), he was also fatally attracted

to boldness of action. People were too blinkered by consider-
ations of morality and caution, he thought. This never
achieved anything. What was required was daring of vision:
the ability to see, and carry through, the larger project. Alas,
this view has its drawbacks. In the heat of the moment, one
vital element can be overlooked: the question of plausibility.

Where a practical project is concerned, this means it ends
in farce. (Hundreds of diggers blundering about in a large
flooded ditch, the sage-in-residence thoughtfully stroking his
beard.) Where theory is concerned, as in Machiavelli's
political theory, no such denouement occurs. The theory can
always remain an enticing project. This was to be the great
attraction of Machiavelli's amoral science of politics: if it failed
in the practical sphere, the perpetrator could be blamed. In
the end, his inadequate application of the theory had let him
down. The theory itself remained intact. Whether it *could* ever
be applied adequately was another matter. Its plausibility
simply wasn't questioned. (This accounts for both the flaws,
and the prevailing popularity, of many political theories
throughout the ages – from utilitarianism to Marxism.
Practical failures in their name can always be blamed on
incompetent or inadequate application.)

Soderini prudently decided to send Machiavelli away on
another long journey. By now a third leading player had
entered the fray of Italian politics. The close of 1507 saw the
Holy Roman Emperor Maximilian I preparing to move his
German armies into northern Italy. Here he had a powerful
ally in the form of Florence's rival, Milan.

Machiavelli was dispatched across the Alps to the imperial
court of Maximilian. (Soderini no longer trusted the resident
Florentine ambassador.) This trip was to take Machiavelli six
months and was to result in a report that revealed a crucial
deepening of his political understanding. In his 'Report on the
German Nation', Machiavelli characterises the Germans as a

serious-minded, thrifty people, also noting their primitiveness and physical strength. This is intended as a salutary contrast to the Italians. (Diplomatic reports are still perforce written in this politically incorrect and racist manner, only nowadays strict precautions are taken to ensure that they are *not* published as literary works.) Machiavelli speaks admiringly of the German city-states, which paid low wages and thus had large budget surpluses. This enabled them to support their own well-equipped militias, which in times of danger could pull together for the sake of the nation. He speaks admiringly of 'the power of Germany, which abounds in men, riches, and arms'. Yet acutely he notes that 'the strength of Germany lies more in its city-states than in its princes'. He also pinpoints a weakness that arose from this. The city-states were strong enough to defend themselves but seldom gave more than lukewarm support to their overall emperor. If the emperor embarked upon an ambitious foreign enterprise, the arrival of troops from the city-states was seldom co-ordinated. 'The city-states understand that any acquisitions made in foreign countries, such as Italy, would be for the benefit of the prince [emperor] rather than themselves.'

On his return from Germany, Machiavelli was at last able to put his own militia into practice. Although his military experience remained strictly theoretical (advice manuals, observations of Borgia, consultations with his famous military engineer-sage, etc.), Machiavelli proved a success as a civilian military leader. He played a major role in directing the retaking of Pisa in 1509.

But the storm clouds continued to gather over Italy. In 1511 Machiavelli was dispatched to the French court, now moved ominously to Milan. Here he did his best to talk the French out of starting a major war. This would have involved the Holy League (Maximilian and the pope), the Spanish, the French, Milan, Venice – and, inevitably, Florence. But the

French refused to listen. 'They do not understand a thing about statecraft,' complained Machiavelli in public. But once again he covertly understood the lesson: when you are the power in power politics, there is no need to negotiate.

Events now moved quickly. The pope declared against Florence, indicating that he favoured reinstating the Medici as rulers of the city. The forces of the Holy League advanced and surrounded Florence. The city militia refused to take on the tough Spanish forces, whereupon the citizens rose in favour of the Medici. Soderini was forced to flee, and Giuliano de' Medici marched into Florence.

This was the end for Machiavelli. Stripped of office (for supporting Soderini), stripped of his citizenship (a deep public humiliation), and fined a thousand gold florins (effectively bankrupted), he was banished from the city and exiled to his small property seven miles south of the walls. Just forty-three, his life was in ruins.

But worse was to come. Four months later, in February 1513, a plot to assassinate Giuliano de' Medici was uncovered. One of the conspirators was found to have a list of twenty leading citizens who might be in favour of their cause if they succeeded. Machiavelli was on the list; a warrant was issued for his arrest.

Machiavelli hears of this and immediately surrenders himself to the authorities so that he can plead his innocence. He is flung into the Bargello, the city's notorious prison. Sitting in his cell, he hears the priests praying as they accompany the howling conspirators to their execution. He trembles in the dark, in a cold sweat, convinced he is next. But first he is subjected to torture, in the form of the *strappado*. The victim's wrists are bound behind his back and tied to a rope which passes over a pulley. He is then hauled above the ground, his entire weight supported by his wrists yanked up behind his back. Then the rope is released so that the victim plunges *almost* to the floor. The jolt of pain is excruciating, with the possibility of the victim's arms being wrenched from their sockets.

Machiavelli is subjected to four doses of the *strappado* – considered customary treatment, part of the service laid on by the penal system. Middle-aged and of unprepossessing physique, Machiavelli nonetheless bears up well under his tortures and is proud that 'I have borne them so straightforwardly that I love myself for it'. Yet there is no doubting the effect on him. His political theory was to place great emphasis on torture. A ruling prince should 'be held in constant fear, owing to the punishment he may inflict'. Pain, and fear of its possibility, are what lie behind moral sanctions, laws, and even treaties. Machiavelli knew what he was talking about, and knew this fear. Here was an extremity of action he *had* experienced.

After two months in the Bargello, Machiavelli was released, and returned in despair to his small country estate. Here he lived in his rambling farmhouse, amidst the beauty of the Tuscan hills, cultivating his olives and vines, supervising the husbandry of his few sheep and goats. After the sun set on his long day, he would retire to the local inn to drink wine, chat with the butcher and the miller, and play cards. Yet he loathed every minute of it. He longed to return to the high life, the world of the committees and the courts, the buzz of power and intrigue. He had been someone who mattered, now he was nobody.

How could he ingratiate himself with the Medici? How could he prove that all he had ever done had been in the interests of Florence – not for any political faction or to slight the Medici? He was a patriot, not a self-seeking man. He wrote begging letters, ingratiating poems, courteous disinterested advice on the matters of the day. These were ignored, as he quietly suspected they would be, though this hardly assuaged his bitter disappointment.

Even so, Machiavelli still had an ace up his sleeve. He had been a man of the world, a man of affairs – he had led missions to the courts of Italy, to the pope, to France, Germany, to kings and emperors. The destiny of Florence had depended upon his skills. He knew how politics worked. Now was the time for him to set down this knowledge, to formalise it. Now was the time to discover the science that he knew lay behind the everyday dealings of politics. He would set down the laws of this science once and for all in a book. And once this book was placed in the right hands, its powerful owner would surely understand the benefits of hiring its author.

Each evening Machiavelli would return from the inn, his worn leather shoes scrunching through the silent darkness around him. Above the black silhouette of his house at the end of the road, the stars prickled the night. 'When I arrived home I would go straight to my study. At the door I would take off my day clothes, which were covered with mud and dust, and put on my court robes. Appropriately attired, I would enter the courts of the past, where I would be affectionately received and sit down to dine on the food to which I was born, which is mine alone. Here I am no longer too timid to ask questions and demand reasons for particular actions, and the voices of the past courteously answer me. For four long hours I feel no weariness and I forget all my troubles. I no longer fear poverty, or am dismayed at the prospect of death. I devote myself entirely to my conversations . . .'

In a white heat of inspiration, Machiavelli completed *The Prince* between spring and autumn 1513. All the learning he had acquired – from books and in the service of the Florentine republic – was fused into a simple but profound practical philosophy. Bitter despair had at last stripped him of all illusion, and he saw, as if for the first time, the pitiless truth that underlay all political life. The vision he described was clear and uncompromising: the world as it is, and always has been.

The Prince is addressed to a prince ruling a state, and advises him on how to maintain his rule as efficiently as possible. This efficiency is Machiavelli's political science. Machiavelli understood that science, as such, is neither ethical nor compassionate. It either works or it doesn't. What he now set down was the way political science worked.

Machiavelli opens by describing the different types of states and how these will affect the way a prince rules them. He also indicates how a prince can conquer a state, and how to hold on to it. For instance, when a prince acquires a state in a region which has a different language, he must take up residence there. This was how the Ottoman Turks had held on to Byzantine Greece. Another approach is to establish colonies in the new territories. 'These serve as fetters in securing the conquered state.' This was how the Romans had secured the different provinces of their empire.

Machiavelli goes on to contrast types of government. He compares Turkey and France as they were ruled in his day. The Turkish Empire is ruled by one man, and everyone else is his servant. He divides his empire into *sandjaks* (administrative regions), supervised by governors, whom he moves about as he sees fit. By contrast, the king of France is surrounded by a group of hereditary nobles, each acknowledged and loved by the subjects of his particular domain. All have their prerogatives and privileges, and the king can strip them of these only at his peril. To make a comparison between these two different types of states: The Turkish Empire will be difficult to take, but once acquired, easy to retain. By contrast, the kingdom of France is in a way easier to conquer but would be much more difficult to retain.

Under the chapter heading 'For Those Who Seize Power by Crime', Machiavelli doesn't hesitate to give advice on cruelty and how to inflict it. 'Cruelties inflicted immediately to secure one's position are well inflicted (if one may speak well of ill).' Note this last proviso: Machiavelli still considered himself moral, even if his advice was not. This is an interesting inconsequence, as difficult to maintain as the English found the bits of France which they frequently conquered. But here it is essential to stress a point in Machiavelli's favour – an obvious one, often overlooked (especially by misguided executives who read *The Prince* for tips on how to succeed in business). Machiavelli's book is advice to a prince on how to run a state. It is not a guide to personal morality. It is aimed at a rare class of people in specific circumstances. Needless to say, this is not how it has been read through the years. Ambitious executives, junior officers, or politicians may have misread Machiavelli's particular message, but they have certainly grasped its implications (which in his anger and despair Machiavelli may have overlooked). Machiavelli is dealing with qualities of leadership. The qualities of ultimate leadership may well be those he describes. Whether these are the qualities of leadership on other levels in other circumstances is another matter. Do these latter-day Machiavellians really wish to end up running an outfit that resembles a Renaissance city-state? On the other hand, Bertrand Russell was absolutely right when he called *The Prince* 'a handbook for gangsters'. Mafia families do resemble Renaissance city-states – in their primitive political methods, though alas not in their cultural sophistication or taste.

But back to the theoretical bloodbath. Machiavelli goes on to recommend: 'When seizing a state the conqueror should consider all the injuries he must inflict, and then inflict them all at once, so that he doesn't have to repeat them day after day. In this way he can set the people's mind at rest, and win them over when he distributes favours.'

This may be perceptive stuff, but it is scarcely timeless wisdom. Only in the second half of this short book does Machiavelli come into his own. Here he describes the virtues a prince must acquire, and the vices he should shun, in order to maintain his rule. This indeed is the main concern: '*mantenere lo stato*' (to hold on to his state), and to do so for as long as possible.

The new ruler should make his rule appear well established and permanent. 'Men should either be treated generously or destroyed, because they are liable to take revenge for small injuries – heavy injuries eliminate this inconvenience.' This leads him to the question: 'Is it better for a leader to be loved, or to be feared?' Machiavelli initially appears to hedge his bets, but he leaves no doubt about his ultimate conclusion: 'It is best for a leader to inspire both love and fear. But because of the difficulty of maintaining both of these at once, it is safer to be feared, if one has to choose.' His understanding of human nature is equally pragmatic: 'As long as most people are not deprived of either property or honour, they remain satisfied.'

Machiavelli insists that the political philosopher should avoid describing the imaginary states and utopias used by earlier writers to embody their ideas. This genre already had an illustrious history, going back to Plato's *Republic*, though its epitome did not in fact appear until 1513 – three years after Machiavelli wrote *The Prince* – when Thomas More's *Utopia* coined this word, which tellingly comes from the Greek for 'no place'. Machiavelli's chosen genre, the book of advice to a ruler, was also a highly popular form in Renaissance times, especially with armchair statesmen seeking employment. But here again Machiavelli begged to differ. The circumstances he describes in *The Prince* are no utopia, nor does he offer the polished optimistic advice of a literary opportunist. Machiavelli insisted on talking about reality – how people really behave, not how they ought to behave.

Unfortunately Machiavelli's idea of reality was city-state politics during one of the most turbulent and amoral periods in Italian history. Hence the unremitting pessimism and nihilism of his approach. But does it make any difference if our idea of political reality is embodied in Cesare Borgia, the mayor of Coot Falls, Idaho, or the United Nations talking shop? Machiavelli is speaking of the extreme situation. This may be viewed either as instructive or as the bedrock reality that underlies all politics. Is *The Prince* of use as a parable, or better viewed as some kind of political subconscious lurking beneath the handshakes and stirring speeches of contemporary politics?

Any answer to such questions must lie in the prince himself. For Machiavelli, how a prince behaves depends upon his personal qualities. This brings us to the key concept of *virtù*. Machiavelli's use of this word should not be mistaken for its usual ethical or religious meaning. Machiavelli's *virtù* (or that which he commended to his prince) has nothing whatsoever to do with the Christian idea of good. It is utterly devoid of faith, hope, or charity. Likewise, it has little to do with the classical ideas of virtue – justice, fortitude, temperance, prudent restraint. Machiavelli's use of the word *virtù* returns to its original roots: *vir* (man) and *vis* (strength), with connotations of virility. *Virtù* is potency, power – closer to the Nietzschean concept of the 'will to power'. It expresses dynamism and strength, the daring required to seize the opportune moment and follow it through without wavering.

Here again Machiavelli recognises that different circumstances will require the prince to exercise different degrees of *virtù*. The more difficult it is for him to maintain his rule, the greater *virtù* the prince will require.

Whenever possible, a new ruler should try and leave things intact. There should be a minimum of interference in well-established institutions; ancient customs should be encouraged; the people should be left to speak their own language. The greater the disruption, the more likely that disruption will continue. The people might get ideas: if disruption brings in one new prince, it could as easily bring in another.

But there will always be the occasional difficult case where a new prince will need to destroy utterly the state he has taken over, in order to secure his rule. Better smoking ruins and a few cowed survivors than no princedom at all – such is Machiavelli's approach here. This illustrates an important point: the welfare of the state is of secondary importance; the prime concern is that the prince continue as ruler. Such blinkered egoism is of course infantile. Sadly, this lack of maturity is all too relevant. Many rulers continue acting out their nursery problems. Hitler, Stalin, Saddam Hussein – such wilful behaviour is the everyday stuff of the kindergarten.

The possibility of the prince living the quiet life and not grabbing all he can, is not considered. (Why not? Because, quite simply, this option was not available among the city-states of Renaissance Italy. Here once again Machiavelli was being a realist in terms of his own time.) Naturally the subjugation of a state by destroying it will require a proportionally greater degree of *virtù*, according to Machiavelli, though this calculus of *virtù* multiplies to an odd answer. The prince with the greatest *virtù* rules over a vast wilderness of devastated cities. (The most virtuous ruler who springs to mind: Genghis Khan.)

Machiavelli's *virtù* is related to two other key concepts that a prince requires if he is to succeed. These are *fortuna* (fate) and *occasione* (opportunity).

Machiavelli reckoned that we are 50 per cent in control of our destiny – the rest is in the hands of *fortuna* (fate). Here, as ever, Machiavelli aims to be a realist. Philosophers (both political and theoretical) ignore the role of *fortuna* at their peril. The more one learns of history, the more one realises that accident is a major player. (As Pascal put it: 'If Cleopatra's nose had been shorter, the entire face of the world would have changed.') And one has only to study the individual biographies of Hitler, Napoleon, or Stalin to see how many times fate played into their hands. But this is precisely the point that Machiavelli goes on to make. *Occasione* (opportunity) is offered by *fortuna* (fate). It is up to the prince to recognise this opportunity offered by fate, and seize his chance. Likewise, he must also do his best to eliminate as far as possible opportunities for rivals to strike against him. As far as possible, *fortuna* must be utilised.

Stoic resignation is the last thing a prince should cultivate – another example of philosophic virtue becoming a princely vice. Indeed, Machiavelli specifically states that a prince 'will find something which seems a virtue may cause his ruin if put into practice, while another thing which seems like a vice may become his saving grace if he sticks to it'. Ruling is not a matter of good and evil but a continuous struggle between forceful *virtù* and the whims of *fortuna*. In line with traditional Italian thinking (and the Italian language itself), Machiavelli understands *virtù* as essentially masculine, *fortuna* as feminine. 'It is better to be impetuous than cautious, because fortune is a woman; and if you wish to control her it is necessary to restrain and beat her.' Modern sensitivities may be offended by this neolithic attitude, but such comic-book stereotyping should not be allowed to obscure the force of what Machiavelli is saying. Positivism is not confined to either gender. (And the harsh reality of power pays lip service to political correctness, at best.)

Fortune favours the brave. Yet 'success or failure lies in conforming to the times'. This means that the prince must be prepared to change his policies according to the circumstances. Hard and fast adherence to principle is bound to lead to ruin. And don't depend on friends, either. A prince 'must rely solely upon himself and his own strength and ability [*virtù*]'. A prince should seek advice only 'when he wants to, not when others want him to'. Machiavelli concludes: 'Popular wisdom has it that some princes who appear prudent are not so by nature, but only because they have been well advised. This is not true. There is one infallible rule: A prince who is not himself wise cannot be well advised – unless he places himself in the hands of a highly prudent man who takes care of all his affairs. In this case he will be well advised, but won't last long. For the man who governs on his behalf will soon take over the state.'

As ever, Machiavelli develops the pessimistic view of human nature. 'Men are ungrateful, fickle cowards, greedy and envious. So long as you succeed they are with you entirely – they will offer you their very soul, their property, even their family. But as soon as you give them nothing to gratify their desires they will turn against you.' Machiavelli even provides a psychological explanation for this: 'The desires of men are insatiable. Their nature urges them to desire all things, but fate permits them to enjoy but a few things. This results in a permanent state of discontent, and causes them to despise what they possess.'

Earlier philosophers, from Plato to St Augustine, had also come to this grim view of human nature. But their pessimism had been tempered by the possibility of redemption (through idealism or Christianity). Having witnessed the behaviour of the pope and the church, Machiavelli dispensed with such sops.

The prince had to remain permanently on his guard – because, as Machiavelli put it, 'the unarmed prophet perishes'. Machiavelli of course intended this literally. Yet he also intended it both as metaphorical advice (that is, the prince should arm himself mentally as well) and as a reference to Savonarola and his fate. Machiavelli's attitude towards Savonarola remained revealingly ambivalent. The cynical lecher and iconoclast in Machiavelli had been opposed to Savonarola's puritan theocratic rule; yet he maintained: 'one should speak of such a great man with reverence'. Savonarola was identified as a man of the spirit; he had no place in politics. Despite the nihilism of Machiavelli's political philosophy, his Christian belief in God remained unquestioned. His philosophy is entirely consistent with Christ's pronouncement: 'Render unto Caesar that which is Caesar's'. (In Italian, Caesar is of course Cesare.) The ruling of the state is unquestionably Caesar's.

Machiavelli and his political philosophy certainly appear utterly amoral. Yet in the perceptive words of the modern Machiavelli par excellence: 'Machiavelli has been invoked for centuries as the incarnation of cynicism. Yet he thought of himself as a moralist. His maxims describe the world as he found it, not as he wished it to be. Indeed, he was convinced that only a ruler of strong moral conviction could keep a steady course while engaging in manipulations on which survival regrettably depended.' Ignoring the obvious element of self-justification, there's little doubt that Henry Kissinger has a point here. This may be called the unspoken element in Machiavelli's philosophy, the understood assumption. Unfortunately, unless they are writ large and clear, such assumptions tend to be overlooked.

In a characteristic parable of deviousness, Machiavelli insists that the prince must behave like an animal. 'He must choose to be like the fox and like the lion. For the lion does not protect himself from traps; and the fox does not protect himself from wolves. Therefore he must be like a fox to protect himself from traps and like a lion to protect himself from wolves.'

With lionlike strength he will deter all threats, both from within the state and outside it. Likewise, he must present himself to the people, and the world, with the cunning of the fox. 'He must leave the affairs of reproach to others, affairs of grace to himself.' If it helps his reputation, he should appear to be good, humane, even merciful. Yet he must always retain fear as an unspoken deterrent. The pomp and circumstance of state, which maintains a distance between the ruler and his subjects, will help him maintain this veneer of nobility and moral rectitude. Those close to him will of course see through this charade, but they will realise the futility of attempting to depose anyone so beloved by his people.

Yet elsewhere Machiavelli maintains: 'He who builds on the people builds on mud.' It is possible to see an inconsistency here. But then, as we have seen, inconsistency is one of the prince's saving virtues. Whether it is such a virtue for a philosopher is another matter. Machiavelli was interested in what worked, not the tidy consistency of ethical or systematic philosophy.

Once again we are faced with one of Machiavelli's implicit assumptions. But here the inconsistency is more disturbing. In *The Prince* Machiavelli has a hidden agenda, which is eventually revealed in all its glory in the final chapter, entitled 'An Exhortation to Seize Italy and Liberate Her from the Barbarians'. (For barbarians, read foreigners. Once again Machiavelli seems to have favoured political realism rather than its correctness.) And the disturbing inconsistency? In his patriotic tirade Machiavelli urges his prince to throw off the foreign yoke and unite Italy, 'bringing honour to himself and prosperity to all the Italian people' (the very same who had earlier been called 'mud'). Included are rousing references to ancient Rome ('the ancient valour of the Italian heart is not yet dead') and to Cesare Borgia ('who seemed ordained by God to redeem Italy'). And Machiavelli says of the prince himself: 'I cannot express with what love he would be received throughout the land . . .' This was the prince who had been instructed how to dupe the people into loving him. Not for nothing did Mussolini write a personal introduction to *The Prince*.

Yet Machiavelli's patriotism is understandable, even if his cynical manipulations are unforgivable. Italy had not been united under Italian rule since the collapse of the Roman Empire well over a millennium earlier. (And it would not be so again until the advent of Garibaldi, more than three centuries later.)

Now we come to the casting of this great epic. Who was to play the star role? Who was to be the prince? Machiavelli dedicated *The Prince* to Giuliano de' Medici, the ruler of Florence. Giuliano was the man who would save Italy. Unfortunately, before Machiavelli could even finish the book, Giuliano ceased to be ruler of Florence. His cousin Lorenzo de' Medici took power. No matter. It was of no real importance *who* led the glorious duped Italians against the 'barbarous stinking tyranny' of the foreigners. What really mattered was the identity of his political adviser. In Machiavelli's opinion there was only one man for this job. The whole point of writing the book in the first place had been to win his way back into favour with the ruler of Florence. (The fact that a work is inspired by several motives does not necessarily invalidate any but the saintly, a category singularly lacking in *The Prince*.)

So Machiavelli simply rededicated his book, making a few pertinent personal changes to the text. Now the 'saviour of Italy' was addressed as '*il magnifico Lorenzo*' (not to be mistaken for the genuine Lorenzo the Magnificent, who had died more than twenty years earlier). Having overcome this little casting difficulty, Machiavelli finished *The Prince* in fine style.

Now he was faced with the problem of delivering his book to its dedicatee, a task fraught with difficulty. Machiavelli was in disgrace and had many enemies at court. He found it impossible to secure a personal audience with Lorenzo. And he knew that if his book fell into the hands of his enemies they would either destroy it or claim his ideas as their own.

It is also worth pointing out that the book itself presents a seemingly insurmountable difficulty for its author in this circumstance. According to Machiavelli, the prince must not be seen to take good advice from others but should claim these ideas as his own. Had Machiavelli succeeded in presenting his book to its dedicatee, we might today be reading *The Prince* by Lorenzo de' Medici.

But this Bacon/Shakespeare problem failed to arise, at least for the time being. Machiavelli remained in disgrace, his efforts to ingratiate himself spurned. Meanwhile he wrote several other works, whose finesse of style was to guarantee him a place in the canon of Italian literature. His play *La Mandragola* (*The Mandrake Root*) is a farce with a cliché plot fit for an opera (virtuous beauty, old husband, young buck, etc.). It was intended as a satire of the louche behaviour of the period, especially among the clergy. Here Machiavelli drew on his own louche social experience.

Machiavelli's *Discourses* are billed as criticism of the great Latin writer Livy and his history of the early Roman Empire. In fact the *Discourses* is another work of political theory. This book was not written in the white heat of despair, and many think it contains a more considered politico-philosophic outlook than *The Prince*, closer to what Machiavelli actually thought. It also differs from *The Prince* in being more plausible, mature, and moderate – unsensational qualities which ensured its eclipse by *The Prince*.

In the *Discourses* Machiavelli states his belief in republican government, especially as practised in the Roman republic.

This time he writes from the citizens' point of view, giving *them* advice on how to run things, especially how to achieve freedom within the state. He follows the principles first laid down by Aristotle: individual freedom and self-government can be achieved only within a state that is also free and self-governing. He believes in collectivism (in other words, when writing for the people he believes in people-power). Surprisingly, in light of his attitude in *The Prince*, he maintains: 'people are more prudent, more stable, and have better judgment than a prince'. Yet one vital element pervades both works: luck, or fate – the one element that always remains beyond all political theory. Machiavelli emphasises that *fortuna* is always required. Just like the prince, the people will also need *virtù*, though here the more Nietzschean, individualistic, unscrupulous element would seem to be shelved in favour of civic virtue, moral fibre, and collective strength.

In 1519 Lorenzo de' Medici died and was succeeded by Cardinal Giulio de' Medici. And at last *fortuna* smiled on Machiavelli. Mindful of Machiavelli's previous experience, Giulio sent him on a minor mission to the nearby city of Lucca. Machiavelli successfully completed his work there and returned to Florence with high hopes. Having demonstrated his loyalty to the Medici, his talents would now surely be put to good use in high office. Instead Giulio appointed him official historian to the republic of Florence, on a salary of 57 gold florins – which at least guaranteed his financial security. Machiavelli hid his disappointment and started on his official task: a history of Florence. In this he faced something of a problem. His *Florentine History* had to be written without offending the Medici, who had played a major and far from blameless part in this history. As Machiavelli put it when advising a fellow civil servant: 'If sometimes you need to conceal a fact with words, do so in such a way that it does not become known. Or, if it does become known, make sure you have a ready and quick defence.' Unfortunately his contemporary and friend, the great historian Guicciardini, was later to reveal many facts which Machiavelli had glossed over – but by then Machiavelli was no longer around to give 'a ready and quick response'. Machiavelli's *Istorie fiorentine* (*Florentine History*) is best read as literature.

In 1523 Giulio de' Medici relinquished his rule of Florence to become Pope Clement VII. These were once again difficult times in Italy. Two years later the balance of power in the Italian peninsula collapsed. Charles V, king of Spain and Holy Roman Emperor, threatened the entire peninsula. Machiavelli was put in charge of the fortification of Florence and then travelled with the army to join Guicciardini, who was lieutenant of the papal forces.

But all to no avail. In May 1527 the army of Charles V sacked Rome. Simultaneously Machiavelli heard that the citizens of Florence had risen against the Medici and established a new republic. Now *fortuna* was really smiling on him. Machiavelli grasped the *occasione* with both hands. He set off posthaste for Florence, confident of being returned to high office at last. But once again he was disappointed. This time he was in disfavour for having *supported* the Medici!

This final setback was too much. Machiavelli fell ill. Still in dire financial straits, and by now despairing, he was attended by his few remaining friends. After having requested and received the last rites, he died the following month, on 21 June 1527, aged fifty-eight.

AFTERWORD

Machiavelli had been devious, scheming, deceitful, and untrustworthy – and in *The Prince* he had advocated this method of behaviour. But in doing so he had also laid bare a certain truth about human nature. This proved a raw nerve. Human nature had to be better than this – no man could ever behave like Machiavelli's prince. This was undoubtedly the work of the devil; all were soon agreed on this (especially the church). Machiavelli quickly became demonised, in a uniquely literal sense. 'Old Nick', a popular name for the devil, derives directly from Niccolò Machiavelli. Likewise, his surname spread through Europe as a byword for evil. Just thirty years after his death his name began cropping up as far afield as England. And before the end of the sixteenth century it was sufficiently recognisable to the public for Shakespeare to use it in *The Merry Wives of Windsor*: 'Am I politic? Am I subtle? Am I a Machiavel?' (Some even claim Machiavelli was the model for Iago in *Othello*.)

But why all this fuss? Unwittingly Machiavelli had put himself in line for a major posthumous role. He became a pawn in the great struggle that split the church and ravaged Europe during the sixteenth and seventeenth centuries, namely, the Reformation. His name came to epitomise the Italian corruption of the church and was used in the propaganda war by the northern European forces that strove to establish Protestantism. (Shakespeare would not have referred to Machiavelli in such fashion if England had remained Catholic.) But was this all?

No. Machiavelli had uncovered an even deeper split. Since the beginnings of philosophy, thinkers had implicitly assumed that human beings were essentially the same. There was such a thing as a universal human nature. This implied an ideal form of society in which all human beings could best live. Plato had attempted to describe this utopia in *The Republic*. Others had suggested ways to improve human society for the good of all concerned. And in the centuries *following* Machiavelli, Enlightenment thinkers, believing in some ultimate harmony of human values, sought basic principles of human nature – and a society in which these principles could be expressed (the United States Constitution is a prime example). More scientific attempts to create similar harmonious societies arose in Marxism, collectivism, and many socialist movements. Indeed, the belief that we can live together in peace, love, and harmony persisted into the 1960s and beyond.

Yet long before all this, Machiavelli had implied the impossibility of such projects. In *The Prince* he suggested the contradiction between running (or serving) a state while at the same time living a moral life. In order to run a state efficiently one had to forget about morality. *The Prince* provoked the question: could a ruler employ such hypocrisy, deceit, and even murder while subscribing to the personal ethics of Christianity? In other words, is it possible to rule without morality and yet remain a moral person?

From the Borgia popes to Pol Pot, history has provided us with only one grim answer to this question. The answer soon became grimly evident. Yet if this was the case, it led to a profound contradiction. As the great twentieth-century political philosopher Isaiah Berlin pointed out, this means we are left with ethical pluralism. There is no objective solution to the problem of how human beings should live. How should we behave? The lack of any answer is deafening – and frightening.

So? Groups of people can, and will, feel the need to form societies in which people live together in largely different ways. Such societies may be fascist, Communist, or democratic, they may include tyrannies or even anarchy. Almost anything is possible. And one only has to search through history – from the auto-destructive bloodbaths of Mayan human sacrifice to the stylite 'communities of hermits' – to become aware of the infinite possibilities of human inventiveness in this matter. Yet there are no common criteria by which a rational decision can be made between the merits of these different societies. If morality and the science of politics are separate, as Machiavelli showed they are, we simply have no yardstick for universal judgment. This means that Hitler's Germany stands alongside parliamentary Britain.

All this is profoundly depressing. Yet it stems from an obvious point, of which we are now all aware in the post-Freudian age. Human psychology is not rational or consistent. On the other hand, any moral system or system of government must be rational and consistent. Personal fulfilment and public experience are thus *bound* to come into conflict.

Machiavelli was the first writer to indicate an unpalatable truth of the human condition. He was not a great philosopher but merely a realistic political theorist. Yet his thinking brought humanity face to face with one of its most profound, and seemingly insoluble, dichotomies.

FROM MACHIAVELLI'S WRITINGS, AND OTHER COMMENTS

It is necessary for anyone establishing a state and setting down its laws to presuppose that all people are evil, and that they will always act according to the wickedness of their spirits whenever they get the chance.

– Machiavelli, *Discourses*

The papacy, too, has never been in a position to carry on Christian politics; and when reformers indulge in politics, as Luther did, one sees that they are just as much followers of Machiavelli as any immoralist or tyrant.

– Nietzsche, *The Will to Power*

Much of the conventional obloquy that attaches to [Machiavelli's] name is due to the indignation of hypocrites who hate the frank avowal of evil-doing.

– Bertrand Russell, *History of Western Philosophy*

Wars begin when you want, but don't end when you wish.

– Machiavelli, *Florentine History*

The only way to protect yourself from flatterers is to make clear to people that you do not mind being told the truth. Yet when everyone can tell you the truth, you lose respect.

– Machiavelli, *The Prince*

One can save one's soul, or one can found or maintain, or serve a great and glorious state; but not always both at once.

– Isaiah Berlin, in his essay on Machiavelli

It is not unlikely that fascism owes its early military-like features to Machiavelli, but it is in the first years in power that Machiavelli's influence on Mussolini was most evident.

– Laura Fermi, widow of the great Italian scientist Enrico Fermi and biographer of Mussolini

Machiavelli was the greatest Italian philosopher ... the teacher of all teachers of politics ... but he did not have enough contempt for humanity.

– Benito Mussolini

Marx defined politics as 'the art of the possible'; two centuries previously Machiavelli had invented realpolitik ...

People should be treated either with generosity or destroyed. They can take revenge from slight injuries – but not from heavy ones.

– Machiavelli, *The Prince*

This throwback to the most cruel Machiavellianism seems incomprehensible to one who until yesterday abided in the comforting confidence that human history moves along a rising line of material and cultural progress.

– Leon Trotsky, in his biography of Stalin

CHRONOLOGY OF SIGNIFICANT PHILOSOPHICAL DATES

6th C BC	The beginning of Western philosophy with Thales of Miletus.
End of 6th C BC	Death of Pythagoras.
399 BC	Socrates sentenced to death in Athens.
c 387 BC	Plato founds the Academy in Athens, the first university.
335 BC	Aristotle founds the Lyceum in Athens, a rival school to the Academy.
AD 324	Emperor Constantine moves capital of Roman Empire to Byzantium.
AD 400	St Augustine writes his *Confessions*. Philosophy absorbed into Christian theology.
AD 410	Sack of Rome by Visigoths heralds opening of Dark Ages.
AD 529	Closure of Academy in Athens by Emperor Justinian marks end of Hellenic thought.
Mid-13th C	Thomas Aquinas writes his commentaries on Aristotle. Era of Scholasticism.
1453	Fall of Byzantium to Turks, end of Byzantine Empire.
1492	Columbus reaches America. Renaissance in Florence and revival of interest in Greek learning.

1543	Copernicus publishes *On the Revolution of the Celestial Orbs*, proving mathematically that the earth revolves around the sun.
1633	Galileo forced by church to recant heliocentric theory of the universe.
1641	Descartes publishes his *Meditations*, the start of modern philosophy.
1677	Death of Spinoza allows publication of his *Ethics*.
1687	Newton publishes *Principia*, introducing concept of gravity.
1689	Locke publishes *Essay Concerning Human Understanding*. Start of empiricism.
1710	Berkeley publishes *Principles of Human Knowledge*, advancing empiricism to new extremes.
1716	Death of Leibniz.
1739–1740	Hume publishes *Treatise of Human Nature*, taking empiricism to its logical limits.
1781	Kant, awakened from his 'dogmatic slumbers' by Hume, publishes *Critique of Pure Reason*. Great era of German metaphysics begins.
1807	Hegel publishes *The Phenomenology of Mind*, high point of German metaphysics.
1818	Schopenhauer publishes *The World as Will and Representation*, introducing Italian philosophy into German metaphysics.
1889	Nietzsche, having declared 'God is dead', succumbs to madness in Turin.
1921	Wittgenstein publishes *Tractatus Logico-Philosophicus*, claiming the 'final solution' to the problems of philosophy.
1920s	Vienna Circle propounds Logical Positivism.

1927	Heidegger publishes *Being and Time*, heralding split between analytical and Continental philosophy.
1943	Sartre publishes *Being and Nothingness*, advancing Heidegger's thought and instigating existentialism.
1953	Posthumous publication of Wittgenstein's *Philosophical Investigations*. High era of linguistic analysis.

CHRONOLOGY OF MACHIAVELLI'S LIFE AND TIMES

1469	Birth of Niccolò Machiavelli in Florence. Lorenzo the Magnificent takes power in the city.
1478	The Pazzi Conspiracy fails; Lorenzo narrowly escapes assassination.
1492	Death of Lorenzo the Magnificent. Columbus reaches America. Alexander VI, father of Cesare Borgia, becomes Pope.
1494	Charles VIII, king of France, leads his troops into Florence. Savonarola takes power in Florence.
1498	Savonarola tried, hanged, and burned at the stake in Florence. Machiavelli elected secretary to the Second Chancery, and later secretary to the Ten of War.
1500	Machiavelli leads mission to France.
1501	Machiavelli marries Marietta di Luigi Corsini.
1502	Cesare Borgia takes Urbino. Machiavelli on mission to Borgia's court.
1503	Borgia murders Vitelli and his fellow conspirators. Death of pope Alexander VI signals decline in Cesare Borgia's fortunes.
1505	Machiavelli establishes Florentine militia.

1508	Machiavelli sent on mission to Germany.
1512	Balance of power in Italy collapses. Florence besieged, Soderini flees, Medici return to power. Machiavelli stripped of office and banished.
1513	Machiavelli implicated in plot to overthrow Giuliano de' Medici. After torture, he is released from prison. Machiavelli returns to his estate and writes *The Prince*.
1523	Giulio de' Medici, new ruler of Florence, sends Machiavelli on minor mission.
1527	Balance of power in Italy once again collapses, and Rome sacked. Medici rule overthrown in Florence. Machiavelli returns, is offered no post, and dies on 21 June.

RECOMMENDED READING

Isaiah Berlin, *The Proper Study of Mankind* (Farrar, Straus & Giroux, 1998). Contains Berlin's great essay on Machiavelli.

Sebastian De Grazia, *Machiavelli in Hell* (Vintage Books, 1994). The latest prize-winning biography, more an intriguing and imaginative meditation on Machiavelli and *The Prince* than a straightforward life.

Niccolò Machiavelli, *Florentine Histories* (Princeton University Press, 1990). Fascinating reading, if sometimes a bit economical with the truth.

Niccolò Machiavelli, *The Prince and Other Political Writings* (Everyman's Library, 1995). The complete text of the masterpiece, with useful footnotes; also includes the pieces of Val di Chiana, Borgia's betrayal, etc.

Pasquale Villari, *The Life and Times of Niccolò Machiavelli*, 2 vols. (Scholarly Press, 1972). Over a century since it first appeared, but still the standard work.

INDEX

A NOTE ON THE AUTHOR

PAUL STRATHERN was educated at Trinity College, Dublin, and lectures in mathematics and philosophy at Kingston University. He has written five novels, one of which won a Somerset Maugham Prize. His most recent works include *Dr Strangelove's Game: A Brief History of Economic Genius* and *Mendeleyev's Dream: The Quest for the Elements*, which was shortlisted for the Aventis Science Prize. He has also written for many journals including the *Observer* (London), *Wall Street Journal* and *New Scientist*. His popular Philosophers in 90 Minutes series is being published worldwide in fifteen languages.